by:

Max Willy

poet, comedian, pervert

A is for anus

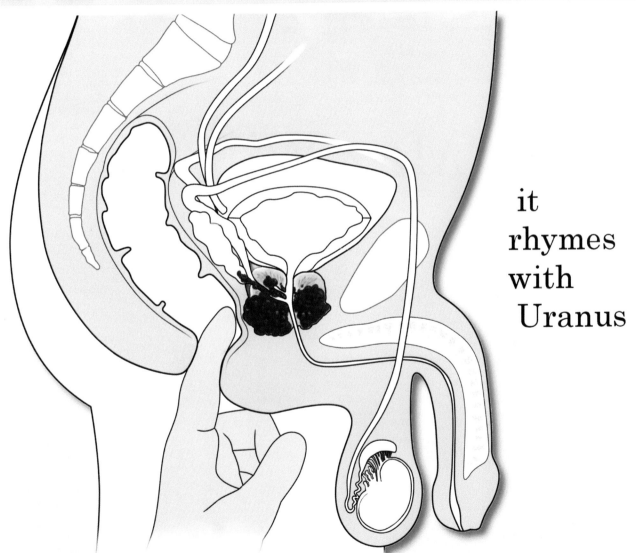

it
rhymes
with
Uranus

B is for butt sex

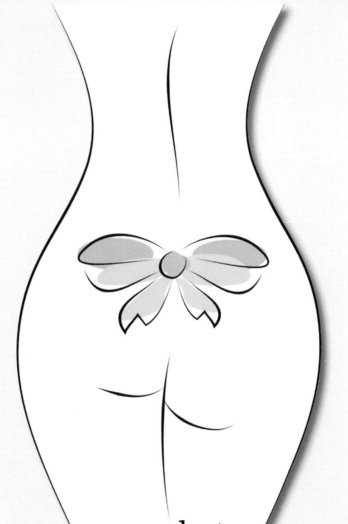

can you guess what cums next?

Condoms

that's right!

remember to use one

or ST...

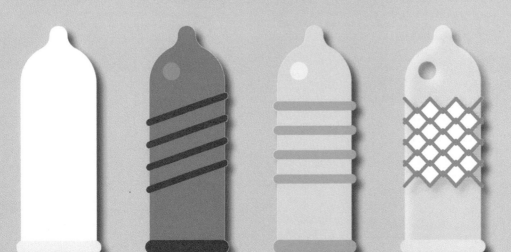

D's

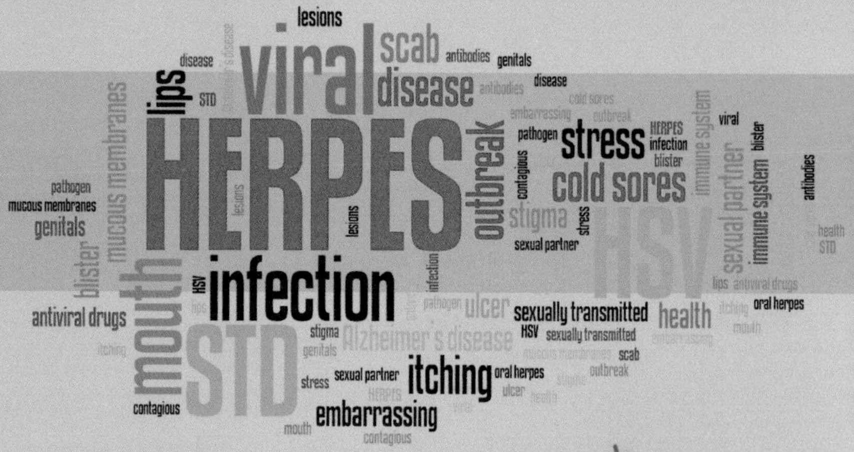

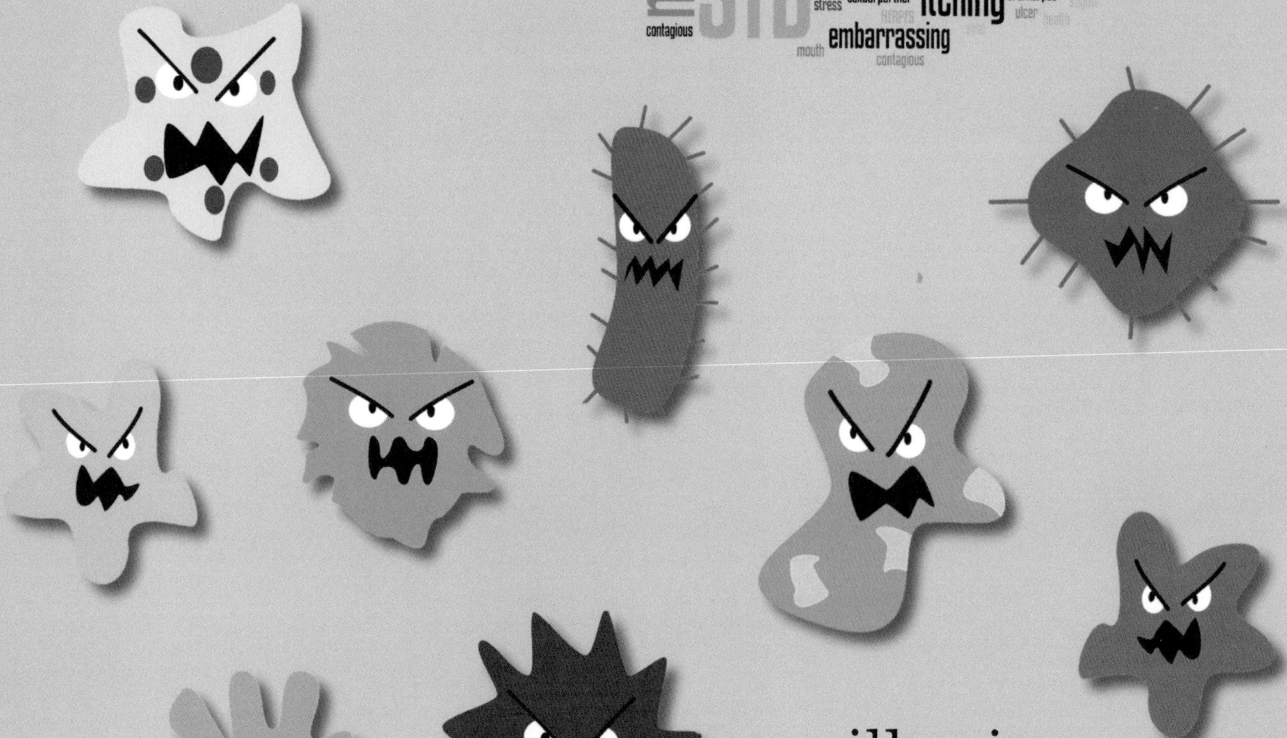

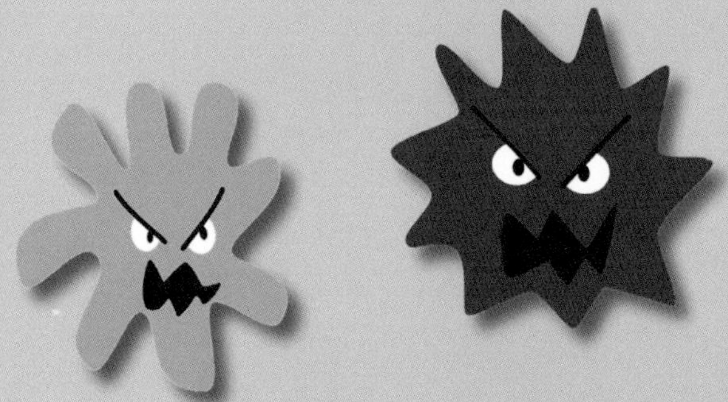

will ruin
all the fun!

get an...

Enema

before you...

Fuck

a duck

on a toy truck

make it...

Gag

make it
wag its tail

rub its...

Happy trail

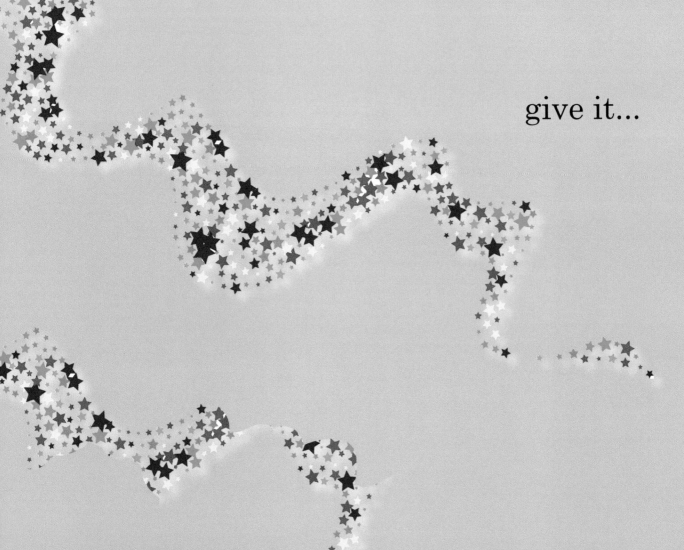

give it...

Ice cream

make it...

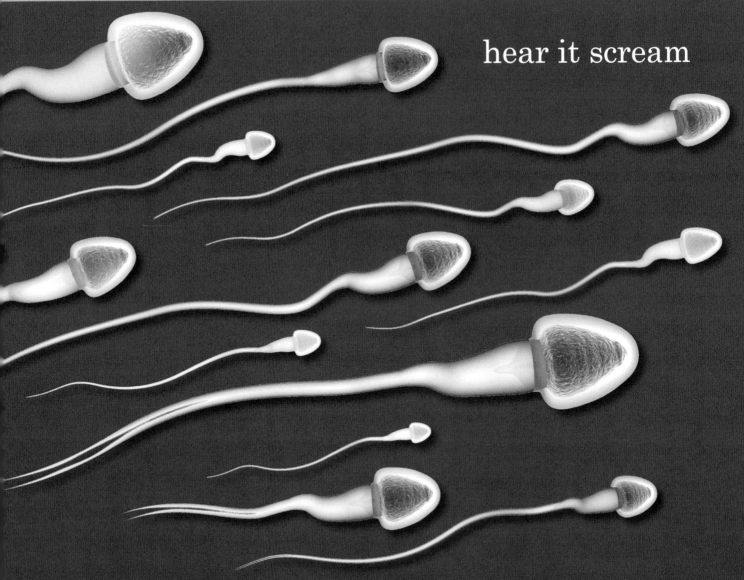

Jizz

hear it scream

take a whizz

all done!

now, where were we?

right...

K is for kinky

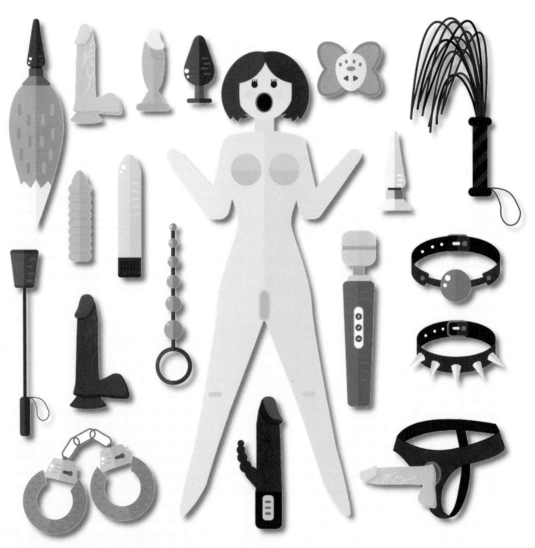

kumquat

 kale

and kiwi

a kundong

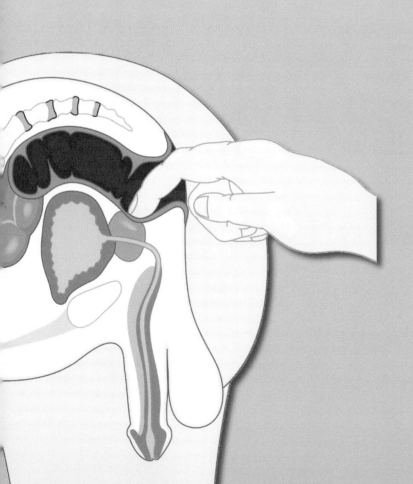

up your
stinky

while
playing
with your slinky!

time for a
geography lesson...

L is for Liberia

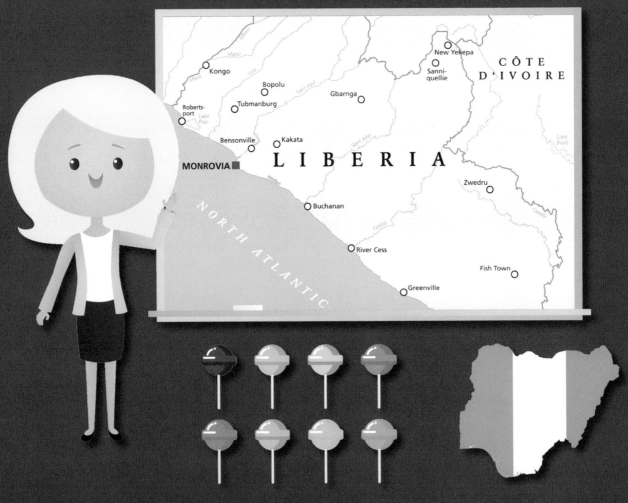

lollipops from Nigeria

Milfs in Siberia

don't meet
my criteria

for...

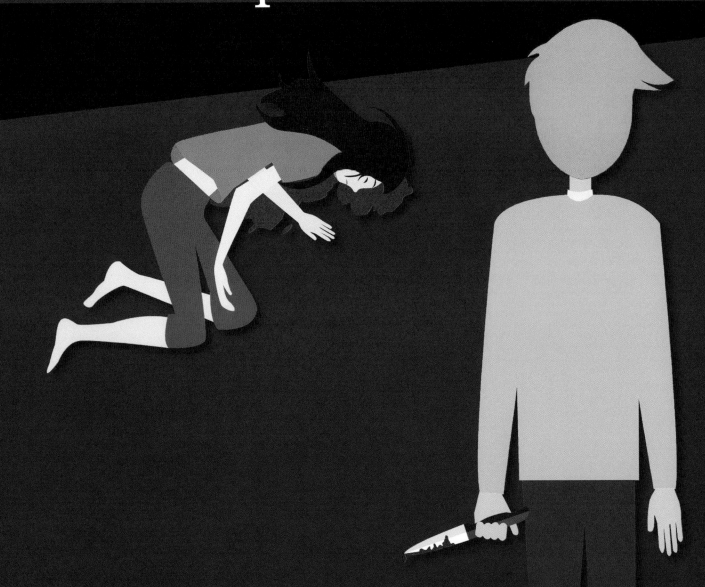

Penis

to Venus

with
Venus de Milo

have a...

Quickie

in Kentucky

Rub one off

in Ohio!

do you love meat?

well then...

S is for salami

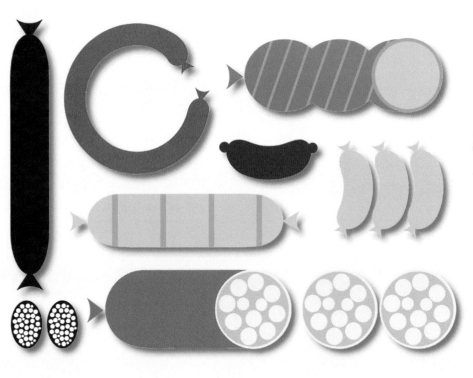

go share some with Tommy

but don't
   tell his mommy

it's not
Origami

stick your...

Tongue

down his throat

lick his...

U vula

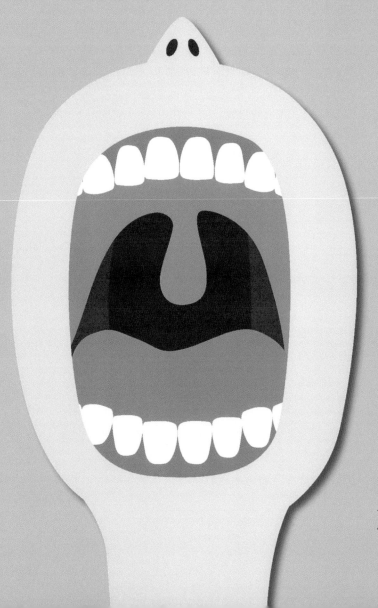

make
him
touch
your...

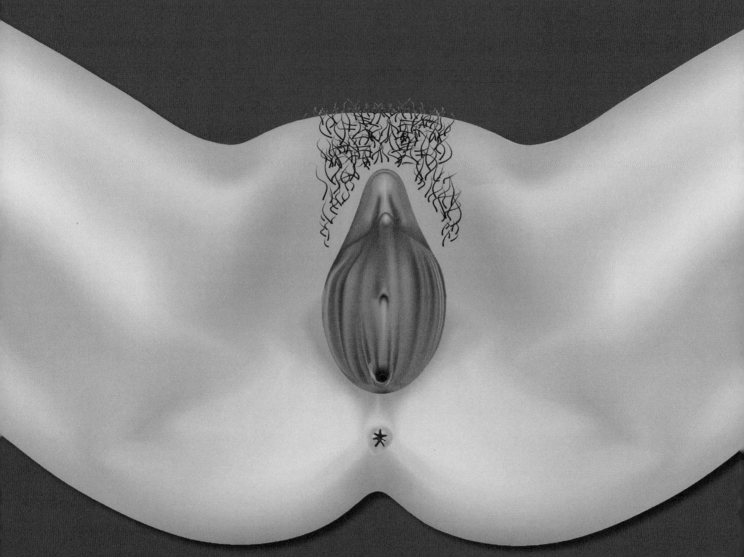

earn your first
cum badge

TOP COCK SUCKER

MAGNA CUM LAUDE

put his...

Wiener

in your schnitzel

watch an...

X-rated movie

make it
drizzle

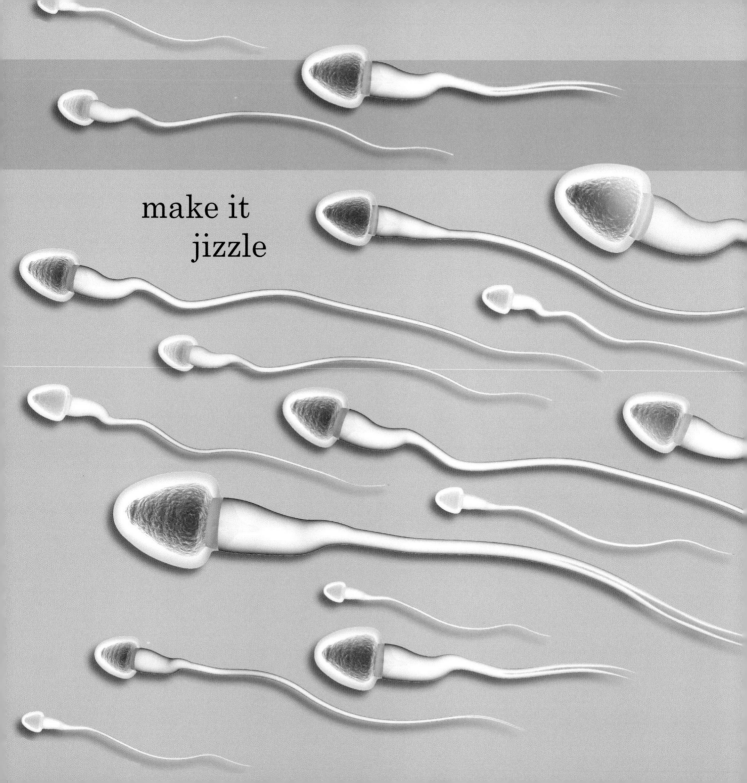

make it
jizzle

Yolo

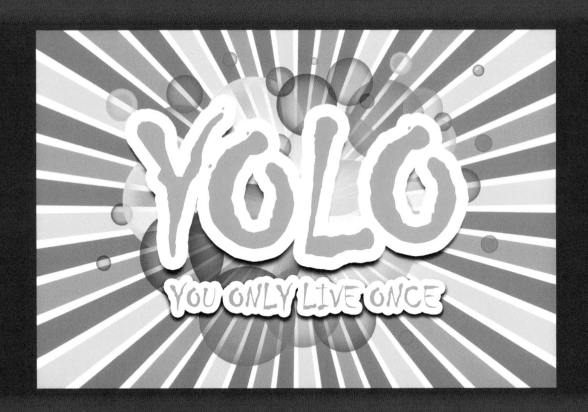

Zip it up

whew!

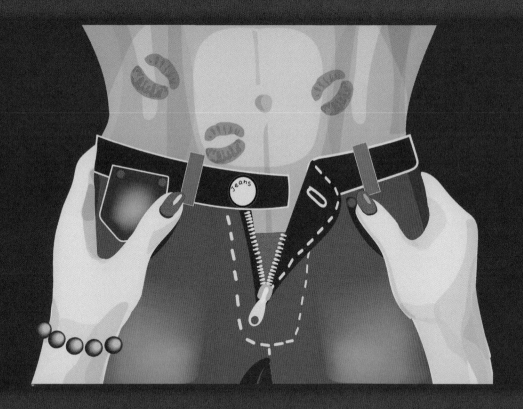

that brings us back to...

A is for anus

which rhymes with
juice

Who is Max Willy?

He is an adult trapped inside a child's body who behaves like a nine-year-old with Tourettes.

As a poet, comedian, and self-proclaimed pervert, he derives much of his humor from the follies of everyday life.

Shakespeare, Voltaire, and pornography are his biggest influences.

Did you enjoy this book?

If so, please leave a review on Amazon, and then punch yourself in the balls or pussy, you naughty, naughty person.

16146658R00026

Printed in Poland
by Amazon Fulfillment
Poland Sp. z o.o., Wrocław